THIS IS THE AMERICAN EARTH~

ANSEL ADAMS: *Sierra Nevada from Lone Pine, California*

This, as citizens, we all inherit. This is ours, to love and live upon,
and use wisely down all the generations of the future.

In all the centuries to come

Always we must have water for dry land, rich earth beneath the plow,
    pasture for flocks and herds, fish in the seas and streams,
    and timber in the hills.

Yet never can Man live by bread alone.

Now, in an age whose hopes are darkened by huge fears—
    —an age frantic with speed, noise, complexity
    —an age constricted, of crowds, collisions, of cities choked by
        smog and traffic,
    —an age of greed, power, terror
    —an age when the closed mind, the starved eye, the empty heart,
        the brutal fist, threaten all life upon this planet—

        What is the price of exaltation?

ANSEL ADAMS: *Nevada Fall, Yosemite National Park*

What is the value of solitude?
—of peace, of light, of silence?

ANSEL ADAMS: *Fern in Rain, Mount Rainier National Park*

ANSEL ADAMS: Lake MacDonald, Evening, Glacier National Park

What is the cost of freedom?

ANSEL ADAMS: Clouds and Peaks, Glacier National Park

ANSEL ADAMS

NANCY NEWHALL

THIS IS THE

ANSEL ADAMS: *Half Dome, Winter, Yosemite Valley*

AMERICAN EARTH

SIERRA CLUB · SAN FRANCISCO

Designed by Nancy Newhall and David Brower. Set in Centaur.
Composition by the Gillick Press, Berkeley. Gravure plates and
printing by Photogravure and Color Company, New York City.
Text Paper is Warren's Offset Enamel Dull. Cover stock is Curtis
Paper Company's Tweedweave. Binding by Sendor Bindery.

The Sierra Club, founded in 1892 by John Muir, has devoted
itself to the study and protection of national scenic resources,
particularly those of mountain regions. Participation is invited
in the program to enjoy and preserve wilderness, wildlife,
forests, and streams. Address: Mills Tower, San Francisco.

FOREWORD

A mile of mountain wall spills out of the Wyoming sky beyond a wide meadow, a meadow edged with wonder this morning when a small boy's excited cry *moose!* woke us and we watched a mother and calf leisurely browse their way downstream, ford, and then disappear into the tangle of cottonwood, aspen, fireweed, and lodgepole. They were not exactly a graceful pair, for nature had something else in mind than mere grace of line when the moose was designed. But they graced the place where we saw them and added to it a new dimension of wildness and of space. A moose needs a lot of wild space and here she found it, in a place that is just about as much the way it was when trappers first saw it as a place could be and still be part of a national park a million people see each year.

It was three years ago that the boy saw his first moose here. Now his age had doubled without a moose's having recrossed his ken; yet he knew exactly, without hesitating a moment, what the cow and calf were, and with no rack of antlers to guide him. The image fixed well, as wild images do, on that perfectly sensitized but almost totally unexposed film of his mind. The same thing would happen to any other small boy, given the chance, and the composite image of a thousand such experiences would enrich his living in the civilized world so thinly separated from the wildness the boy was designed to live with.

But where will the chance to know wildness be, when this boy is himself a father, when a generation from now he is seeking out a place in which to expose his own six-year-old to wonder? How much of the magic of this, the American earth, will have been dozed and paved into oblivion by the great feats of engineering that seem to come so much more readily to hand than the knack of saving something for what it is?

Man's marks are still few here, but they are being made faster and faster. The cabin hewed with patient care has mellowed and the road to it has not burgeoned beyond the two tracks that led there when it was new. The stream has claimed the bridge that once crossed it; twenty-year-old pines grow on one of the approaches and beavers have built and used and abandoned a lodge on the other. The power line is hardly more permanent than the rail fence that fell and now moulders in the meadow. The highway is so far away that the drone of cars can hardly be heard above the stream music. Silence closes in soon after the sightseeing planes pass by the front of the great range.

But each year these silences are briefer. The throng that comes grows larger, needs more, and forest and meadow make way to accommodate them. Wider highways speed people through faster and crowd out the places where the cow has dropped her calf for all the generations since the ice retreated, and where the trumpeter swan could inform her cygnets of those few things the evolutionary force had not already told them. Here where the blue vault arches over the wildest and least limited open space and beauty, even here man's numbers are taming and limiting with greater and greater speed, heedless of the little losses which add up to deprivation.

Again and again the challenge to explore has been met, handled, and relished by one generation— and precluded to any other. Although Thomas Jefferson argued that no one generation has a right to encroach upon another generation's freedom, the future's right to know the freedom of wilderness is going fast. And it need not go at all. A tragic loss could be prevented if only there could be broader understanding of this: that the resources of the earth do not exist just to be spent for the comfort, pleasure, or convenience of the generation or two who first learn how to spend them; that some of the resources exist for saving, and what diminishes them diminishes all mankind; that one of these is wilderness, wherein the flow of life, in its myriad forms, has gone on since the beginning of life, essentially uninterrupted by man and his technology; that this, wilderness, is worth saving for what it can mean to itself as part of the conservation ethic; that the saving is imperative to civilization and all mankind, whether or not all men yet know it.

Ansel Adams probably knew this in his marrow when he first began to capture the image of wilderness with his camera. Wilderness, let's say, responded unstintingly to this understanding; if a cloud were needed for a given composition, or a highlight or a lowlight, wilderness would provide it, in exactly the right place, to reveal not only breadth and width, but depth and feel too.
The symbiosis went uninterrupted for some twenty-five years and led to this book's conception. The book was assisted when the National Park Service expressed a wish that something functional be done with the little building the Sierra Club had in Yosemite Valley as a memorial to Joseph LeConte, a pioneer conservationist. Ansel Adams suggested an exhibit of photographs and text that would combine to explain what national parks were really all about.

He was offered substantial help by Walter Starr and the California Academy of Sciences and asked Nancy Newhall to lend, "just for a week or two" he thought, her skill with exhibits and text so apparent in her work with the Museum of Modern Art and in her books. She felt an immediate need to bolster her understanding of the conservation force and its origin. One good reference led to another, each revealing still more about that force—and about still more references—until the text could give the exhibit such scope that both artists knew that a book must emerge too. But first Nancy Newhall would go back still further into the collection of great photographs and the record of important ideas, then come back through them, selecting, compressing, arranging, and restating, at last achieving a stirring counterpoint of images, on film and in word, that can reveal in the whole what all the parts could only suggest.

The exhibit itself, although it has turned out to be only a prelude, enjoyed a world-wide audience through the offices of the Smithsonian Institution and the United States Information Agency. New philanthropy helped transform the exhibit into the present book—the combined generosity of Max McGraw and the McGraw Foundation and of the late Marion Randall Parsons, who throughout her life was deeply interested in what the Sierra Club published.

This is the American Earth epitomizes what the Sierra Club, since its founding in 1892 by John Muir, has been seeking on behalf of the nation's scenic resources and needs to pursue harder in the time to come. The book is by far the most important work the club has published and the debt is enormous to Ansel Adams for his inspiration of the book, his photographs, and his guidance, and to Nancy Newhall for the organization of the book and the power of its text. It is a stirring book.

It needs to be a stirring, stirring of love for the earth, of a suspicion that what man is capable of doing to the earth is not always what he ought to do, of a renewed hope for the wide spacious freedom that can remain in the midst of the American earth, at least spacious enough, in the uncounted years, for a moose to drop her calf and coax it far down along the stream to browse and splash and play and lead a small boy to wonder.

DAVID BROWER
Executive Director, Sierra Club

Lupine Meadows, the Tetons,
August 23, 1959

ACKNOWLEDGMENTS

This book, like the exhibition on which it is based, is a sum of dedications: To the many friends who made available their experience with this many-sided problem, and I am thinking here especially of the late Bernard De Voto, whose kind and practical response was to open more doors to more facts and more people; to the poets, historians, philosophers and scientists, from Isaiah and Plato down through Thoreau, Marsh, Muir, and Pinchot to Aldo Leopold, Robert Marshall, Harrison Brown, John Kenneth Galbraith, and many others who, together with their severest critics and most implacable foes, are this book's intellectual progenitors. To our collaborators in the exhibition—Frann and Dick Reynolds, Eldridge T. Spencer, Sam Provenzano; to the photographers who responded so instantly and generously with both prints and negatives; to the George Eastman House for making available historic photographs from their collection, and to American Trust Company, Bishop National Bank of Hawaii, Polaroid Corporation, and the Standard Oil Company of New Jersey for permission to reproduce photographs from their files; to the California Academy of Sciences, which built the first two shows and gave the opening in May 1955 at the Academy in San Francisco; to the M. H. de Young Memorial Museum of San Francisco which lent Greek and Egyptian objects; to the Smithsonian Institution which circulated the show in the United States, and the United States Information Agency which circulated four duplicates overseas; to the artists and craftsmen who have helped, far beyond the call of duty, to make these presentations beautiful, Lawton Kennedy, printer, and Lenscraft Studios, exhibition makers. And now for the book—to Robinson Jeffers for permission to quote lines from *The Bloody Sire*; to Gillick Press of Berkeley and Photogravure and Color Corporation of New York, to conservationist Max McGraw and the McGraw Foundation who made this publication possible. To all these, our deep appreciation.

A.A., N.N.

CONTENTS

PHOTOGRAPHERS

1. BRIEF TENANT

Out of the vast depth of time past, Man comes like a meteor's flash.

In myth, in dream, this living dust remembers

chaos, the drift through endless night, the longing to cohere,

— the shock, the winds, the vast light of Creation.

Was it seven billion years ago this planet formed from the cosmic cloud?

How many billion when first life stirred in the seas?

Our blood is sea water: it remembers tides, the moon's pull.

In the hollow of the womb each of us is life evolving from the sea.

MINOR WHITE: *Rock Pool*

We remember bleak rock and tides of molten fire.

We remember dragons.

What were we when we saw a phoenix hatch in flame, a serpent fly

bright-winged across the sun?

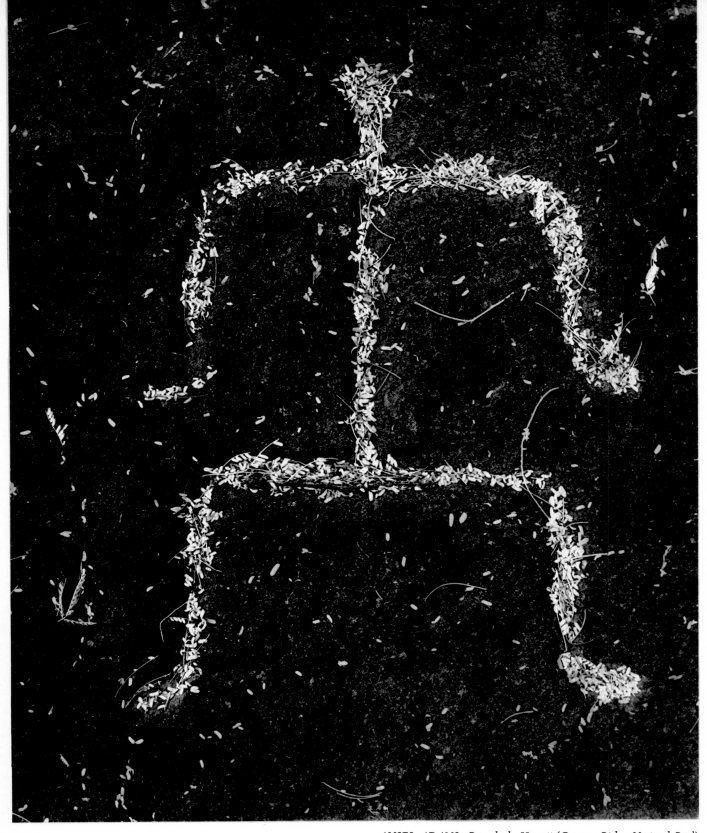

ANSEL ADAMS: *Petroglyph, Hawaii (Courtesy Bishop National Bank)*

Was it only a million years ago that, as man, we first stood upright
and walked with both hands free — to move, to shape, to hurl?
    Ah, we remember Eden! — the radiant vernal earth to which we
        waked as king!
    Why lost, that joy, abundance, freedom?
    Was it the evil Lillith, the lovely Eve? The snake, the tree, the
        fatal knowledge?
    What was our sin? Why, avenging angel?
    O strange creation! Why should new forms of love, evolving, demand
        new forms of death?

Was it only a hundred thousand years ago when, with fire and tools,
as hunters in all continents we began to change life's balances?
  We remember ages of ice; we remember Prometheus,
      bringer of fire from heaven, shaper of strange and deadly tools;
      we remember him bound to a crag, prey to eagles of remorse.
  Survivors of the flood, we remember the rainbow and the dove.

Was it less than twenty thousand years ago when, with game grown scarce
and hunts too long, we turned to the young birds and beasts we petted by
our hearths and bred our flocks and herds?
  We remember the blessing: their increase and our own.
  We remember the bitter sacrifice of the first-born.
  We remember that from drought and desert good shepherds led us to
      green pastures beside still waters.

Was it only six thousand years ago that beside great rivers—
      the Nile, the Tigris and Euphrates, the Yellow, the Indus—
      we began to build cities? To raise with wedge and lever stone
          on stone?
  Conceived the wheel, the forge, the word?
  Learned to time the rising stars?

Was it only eight thousand years ago when we thought to save wild seeds for
planting in the spring?
  No longer wanderers, tethered now to earth,
  praying now for sun, rain, harvest, praying that from winter's death
          should come the resurrection of the spring,
  we remember Osiris, Baldur, Adonis, mourning that for the seed's
          renewal a god must die.

FRANCIS FRITH: *Colossi, Nubia (Collection George Eastman House)*

Brief tenant!

Already across the continents Man's record of ruin lies very old.

In Egypt, thousands of years ago, a crowded, starving people rose
against tyranny; a scribe noted:

> *"The face is pale . . . Robbery is everywhere.*
>
> *The Nile is in flood, but no man plows for himself because every man says,*
>
> > *'We do not know what may happen throughout the land.'*
>
> *Many dead are buried in the river. The stream is a tomb . . .*
>
> *Nobles are in lamentation, while poor men have joy . . . Everytown says, 'Let us banish many from us.'*
>
> *Dirt is throughout the land. There are really none whose clothes are white in these times . . .*
>
> *The river is blood. If one drinks of it, one rejects it as human and thirsts for water . . .*
>
> *Laughter has disappeared . . . It is wailing that pervades the land.*
>
> *The children of nobles are dashed against the walls. The once-prayed-for children*
>
> > *are now laid out on the high ground . . ."*

In Mesopotamia, three thousand years ago, empires had been forgotten and
abandoned cities were falling into mounds.

> Already sands were drifting through the shells of civilizations.

JAMES ROBERTSON: The Acropolis, Athens (collection George Eastman House)

WERNER BISCHOFF: *Famine, India*

In Rome, three centuries after Christ, the Christian Tertullian observed:

> *All places are now accessible . . . all open to commerce . . . cultivated*
> *fields have subdued forests; flocks and herds have expelled wild*
> *beasts . . . Sandy deserts are sown, marshes are drained, rocks are*
> *planted . . . Everywhere are houses, and inhabitants, and settled*
> *governments, and civilized life. What most frequently meets the*
> *view is our teeming population; our numbers are burdensome to the*
> *world . . . our wants grow more and more keen, and our complaints bitter*
> *in all mouths, whilst nature fails in affording us her usual sustenance.*
> *In very deed, pestilence, and famine, and wars, and earthquakes have*
> *to be regarded as remedy for nations, as means of pruning the*
> *luxuriance of the human race.*

In Mongolia, thousands of years ago, sheep herded by men ate dry the lush pastures and reedbeds; lakes vanished, and the soil was lifted by the wind. From this desolation, in years of drought, savage hordes rode forth, age after age, to burn, loot, slaughter.

In China, centuries ago, hungry multitudes stripped bare the hills of the North. Down gullies yearly more cavernous the floods poured until the Yellow River burst its dykes and drowned millions on the plains below.

In India, rich, wasted land; in cycles almost predictable, the specter of famine walked as it still walks, vast and terrible, abroad.

From fallen Rome—
>from ruins once cities ringing the Mediterranean
>from deserts that once shone deep with wheat, and stony slopes once
>>terraced, silver with olives, glowing with grapes
>from hot bare hills once shadowed by oaks and pines long since, as
>>Rome's galleys, sunk beneath the sea
>from fetid marshes, harbors choked with silt, and empty holes once
>>pools reflecting sky—
the barbarous conquerors turned back to their forests in the North
>to build a civilization aspiring to heaven, doomed to war.

Was it five hundred years ago that Man's strange genius, desperate,
dreaming of new means to live, turned to try
>—to harness the invisible, the intangible, the forces known by Satan,
>>prince of the powers of the air
>—to delve deep down for fuels, ores, metals, unknown except to
>>alchemy
>—to sail, to search for wealth beyond all known horizons on this
>>sphere
>—to fly, to catch the lightning in his hand?
>—to conceive a universe no longer centered upon Man, Earth, nor this
>>near star, the Sun?

We remember Faust, and dread his bargain as our own.
We remember the actual Leonardo, far surpassing legend,
>painting sublime ideals of divine intelligence and love,
>sketching in secret the dynamics of water, air, earth, and fire,
>and meanwhile designing dread machines for war.

CLARENCE KENNEDY: Renaissance Man

From an exhausted, exasperated Europe—
from an age of the dance of death, of breaking faiths,
  an age when even the memory of wilderness had vanished
    and the only hope of freedom lay in conquest,
on the third of August, 1492,
Christopher Columbus "stood out to sea a little before sunrise."

2. NEW WORLD

Being thus arrived in a good harbor and brought safe to land,

they fell upon their knees and blessed the God of Heaven . . .

They had now no friends to welcome them,

nor inns to entertain nor refresh their weatherbeaten bodies . . .

And for the season, it was winter . . .

What could they see but a hideous and desolate wilderness,

full of wild beasts and wild men? . . .

If they looked behind them,

there was the mighty ocean which they had passed,

and was now as a main bar and gulf

to separate them from all the civil parts of the world.

— William Bradford, 1620

Here still was Eden—this northern continent which, from shore to shore,
  for many thousand years, red men had kept a hunter's paradise,
Here, few in number, they lived on the wild earth lightly,
  shifting their shelters with the seasons,
  to tend some patch of corn and squashes in summer,
  to watch in winter for moving herds of game.

To this new world in hope and hunger white men came—
  How could we see beauty in this wilderness, with eyes unused,
  and blind with tears for home?

To shape this savage country to our memories,
  we built another Europe—felled trees, burned the forest clear,
  plowed the woodland soils, loosed our strange horned beasts to graze.
  To live, while civilization grew, we learned from red men
  to track wild turkeys in the snow and hunt raccoons on moonlit beaches,
  to net from bays and rivers glittering with fish in spring, uncounted
    multitudes of shad and salmon,
  to shoot into the skies at flights of wildfowl so vast they darkened day.

ANSEL ADAMS: Mortar Holes, Yosemite National Park

Here in this rich continent, we found no man need serve another.
Here any man with ax and gun could live,
clear his own fields, hew his own home, win for himself
a long-forgotten birthright — independence.
Here, in these raw clearings, stirred ideas, ideals
that were to trouble empires;
I infer that the sovereign, original and foundation
of civil power lies in the people.
— Roger Williams, 1644

The natural equality of men *among men must be duly favored,*
in that government was never established by God nor nature
to give one man a prerogative to insult over another . . .
The end of all good government is to promote the happiness
of all and the good of every man
in all his rights to life, liberty, estate, honor, etc.,
without injury or abuse to any.
— John Wise, 1717

Here, in this rich wilderness, we dreamed
that over the next ridge, beyond the next stream
freedom lay forever.

ANSEL ADAMS: *Moro Rock, Sequoia National Park*

CEDRIC WRIGHT: *Stump in Thunderstorm*

Slowly we lost our fear, our blindness; exiles no longer,
we were born to native this earth.

To a boy named Jonathan Edwards there came—

> *sometimes a kind of vision of being alone in the mountains*
> *or some solitary wilderness . . . wrapt and swallowed up in God . . .*
> *Divine glory seemed to appear in everything;*
> *in the sun, the grass, in the water and all nature . . .*
> *I felt God, if I may so speak, at the first appearance of a thunderstorm . . .*

More and more of us came to love wide solitudes
  to see at twilight no hearthlight but our own
  to hear the circle of night's music broken by no housedog's bark
  to seek and savor wildness.

Scout, trapper, explorer, priest, often in fear and hunger, suddenly
topped a rise—
  and heard Niagara roaring in the wilderness
  saw the Tetons dark with thunder
  beheld huge fountains boiling from crystalline craters.
From the great skies and far horizons they returned, reluctantly,
  to civilization and the smallness of a house.

ANSEL ADAMS: The Tetons, Thunderstorm

ANSEL ADAMS: *Cross, Truchas, New Mexico*

When corn grew poor in the clearings, the rivers muddy,
    and game scant in the forests,
When settlement came too close and its noisy road snaked at our heels—
    we moved on West, again to fell, burn, plow, kill.
Why should we heed, how could we hear, the warning voices?
The presidents, naturalists, philosophers, travelers—
    where were they when we heard the wolves howl? the warwhoops rising?
    When we dug the graves and wintered in sod huts?
    When we looked from a height and saw no end to forests or to prairies?
    The wilderness, we knew, was inexhaustible.

ARTHUR ROTHSTEIN: *Clearing*

Farther and farther West, higher and higher among its peaks,
  the mountain men were trapping beaver;
All up and down the Pacific Coast, men in boats were slaughtering
  sea otters; fortunes were being made in fur.

Across the plains and prairies, red men for thousands of years had hunted
  buffalo—their food, fuel, shelter, clothing—yet still the wild herds
  flowed like a black tide.
But now white hunters, in delirious chase, were shooting the buffalo
  down by hundreds, thousands, often merely to kill or take at most
  the tongues.

George Catlin, painting the Plains Indians beyond the Missouri in 1832,
foresaw that they, along with the buffalo, were doomed unless both were
  by some great protecting policy of government, preserved in all
  their pristine beauty and wildness in a magnificent park—
  a nation's park.

BOORNE and MAYS: Sarcee Indian, 1891 (collection George Eastman House)

Back East, by now, most of the wilderness was gone.

Thoreau, seeing the forests falling, cried: "Thank God they cannot cut
      down the clouds!" and asked: "Why should not we . . . have our national
      preserves . . . for inspiration and our true recreation? Or shall we,
      like villains, grub them all up, poaching on our own national
      domains?"

And Emerson, feeling that as new men in a new age, we must turn to Nature,
      not the past, to find our way, was calling on us to look at nature
      with "new eyes."

A new esthetic, that the wilderness is beautiful, was being born.

Scientists, exploring, recording, measuring, testing, began to see
facts forming a theory of Creation more vast, ancient and marvellous
than any myth.
      Before their eyes, beneath their feet, daily the evidence was
      vanishing—some testimony of stone erased, the last survivor
      of some strange species killed.
A new concept, that Nature is wiser and nobler than Man,
was shaping art, philosophy, science.

Already to the last of the East's wild beauty—the Adirondacks, the White
      Mountains, Maine—Easterners were journeying as to shrines.

Already, back East, cities were crowding out upon the farms—
      walls shutting from sun the orchards still forlornly blossoming
      pavements closing over sewers that once were brooks
      factories, yearly larger, noisier, smokier, were destroying shorelines,
         polluting air and water.
No more, after work, could city men and women stroll under evening
      trees and smell the summer meadows under dew.
No more, at morning, could a city child go down to the huge bright
      ocean world, nor, in that ark on earth, a farm, find under feathers the
      warm oval of an egg, nor under leaves ripe hanging forms of
      fruit.

JACOB RIIS: Bandits' Roost, Lower East Side, New York City, 1888
(Collection Museum of the City of New York)

Already, from cities, to reach mere green peace, clear water, pure air,
    we needed more than legs; we needed horses, omnibuses, trains.
Already, in cities, the few small parks were worn bare.
    Walt Whitman, in 1846, reported a Fourth of July celebration in City:
        ... amid dust, danger, obscenity, confusion, deafening din,
        an atmosphere of pulverized impurities, women frightened,
        children crying, rampant, vileness, precocious sin, and
        every phase of the iniquity which springs from the root,
        civilization—there went off their fireworks.

—This, in a continent where no man had built before!

ANSEL ADAMS: *Yosemite Valley, Thunderstorm*

From the West came tales told by scouts, soldiers, settlers, of unbelievable places—
    of a valley called Yo Semite down whose huge precipices many waterfalls
        fell hundreds, thousands of feet—
    of trees huge at the base as houses, trees like towers dwarfing the pines around them—
    of a marvelous hell, steaming, roaring, erupting, in the Yellowstone.

Surveys ventured to these places; photographers confirmed their findings.
Louder and louder came demands that such wild splendors be set aside as parks.

In 1864, Abraham Lincoln signed the Act of Congress deeding to the State
    of California, Yosemite Valley and the Big Trees of the Mariposa Grove,
    as the first park set aside for its beauty,—"to be held inalienable forever."

In 1871, a group of men around a campfire in the Yellowstone decided that
    the awesome phenomena they had seen must never be profaned by commercial
    use, not even by themselves; these must become the nation's heritage.

In 1872, Congress created the Yellowstone the first National "Public Park
    or pleasuring ground for the benefit and enjoyment of the people."

ANSEL ADAMS: Old Faithful Geyser, Yellowstone National Park

Thus, in awe and humility, in foreboding, out of an instinct old as life,

which six thousand years of civilization might warp but not destroy—

heralded from the mountains, began a new relation between Man and the earth.

3. THE MACHINE AND A NEW ETHIC

Beside ox or horse, Americans had walked three thousand miles to the Pacific.

With long rifle, ax and plow, we had conquered a continent.

Now, with the easy riches gone—the furs, the timber, and the gold—

    we stood on the land's last ramparts.

Was this the ending of our dream of freedom? The end of Eden?

MINOR WHITE: Ax and Plowed Field, Oregon

GURNSEY: Wagon Train, Rocky Mountains, c. 1868

SAVAGE: Railroad Across the Plains, c. 1868

Now to our ears came rumor of marvels—of scientists, while sighting their
      huge strange universe, discovering new elements, syntheses, energies, dynamics.
Already in steam we held explosion an uneasy captive;
      already the lightning bore our messages.
Already we had machines—
      machines shrinking a day's labor into hours, shrinking distances in time,
            easing old aches, fulfilling old dreams of speed and power;
      machines replacing hands, coming between us and soil, plant, animal,
            weather, loosening our old closeness to the earth;
      machines involving more machines, founding new industries,
            demanding new ores, fuels, technologies.
Reckless, we tore at the last great virgin resources.
      What did it matter what we wasted or exhausted?
      Science would always save us—find new resources,
            invent new ways for us to live.
We saw before us a new kind of civilization—one, we thought, which through
      the mind of Man we could expand forever.

BILL SEARS: *Cattle Driving, Arizona*

RAY ATKESON: *Log Pond, Oregon*

ANONYMOUS: *Hydraulic Mining*

Miners flung aside pick and pan when free gold in the streams grew scarce,
    and washed gold from the hills with giant hoses. Drilling for oil,
      digging for coal and copper, we bored, blasted, dumped, devastated.
Lumbermen invaded any forest, felled it flat, dragged logs down slopes
    that winter soon eroded; left slash that summer dried to tinder;
      fires roared unchecked, burning mile after mile to barrenness.
Fishermen trawled and trapped such hauls of fish and shellfish
    that even from the seas their nets were coming empty.
Stockmen drove vast flocks and herds over the Western range
    until it was eaten dry, broken by hooves, gullied by torrents.

ANSEL ADAMS: *Overgrazing, California*

PHILIP MILLER: *Duck Hunting*

Market gunners with fumes, flares, snares, and automatic guns, brought down
    uncounted millions of ducks, geese, curlews, pigeons; heaped their wagons
    and left the rest to rot; slaughtered whole rookeries of egrets for their plumes;
    slew for their down all but the last few trumpeter swans.
Hunters killed for the joy of boasting: the bighorn sheep, buffalo, bear, elk,
    caribou, antelope were almost gone.

Farmers ignored strange soils and climates; plowed up and down the hills;
    broke the windswept plains; planted soil without rest or manure
    to the same money crops—corn, cotton, wheat, tobacco—
    and left the furrows bare for winter rains to leach.

CHARLES ROTKIN: *Eroding Farm, Oklahoma*
(courtesy Standard Oil Company)

Havoc descended from the naked hills —

    rains that once fed forests now clawed bare slopes,

    and rivers that once flowed brimming all the year

    and gently, like the Nile, rose each spring to renew their valleys,

    now raged after storms and meltings, tore out their beds,

    undercut their banks, overwhelmed lowlands with sudden floods,

    and left their channels dry in summer heats.

George Marsh, observing that after fifteen centuries the lands Rome ruined

    still lay barren, searched through many tongues and ages

    for records of Man's impact on the earth's dynamics. In 1864 he warned:

        Man has too long forgotten that the earth was given him for usufruct alone,

        not for consumption, still less for profligate waste . . . Let us be wise in time!

U.S. FOREST SERVICE: Burnt Forest

To stop ruin, to save the nation, became for hundreds, thousands, millions

of Americans a cause beyond politics —

    Presidents, housewives, scientists, architects, sportsmen, farmers, businessmen,

    more and more of us, wrote, shouted, pleaded

    — formed societies to learn, explore, act

    — bought with our own funds threatened regions; set up sanctuaries

        for birds and beasts in peril of extinction

    — endowed universities to study the nascent sciences of life

    — urged cities to plan their growth, make spacious parks, curb industrial wastes

    — stormed State legislatures and finally Congress into closing the forests,

        halting destruction, setting up surveys to advise us.

Then conflict old as the snake in Eden split us.

From Europe, where, since before Columbus, nations in dire need

had been planting forests, Gifford Pinchot brought the concept of perpetual yield:

how resources we considered wild—timber, wildlife, pasture, fish—

could be farmed, increased, improved, for use forever.

For this concept he fought to open all closed forests and inviolate parks.

Thousands believed with him there was no nobler concept than material use:

why, in a universe designed for Man, should any hawk soar and circle?

any wild meadow blossom ungrazed, or any great tree fall from age,

unfelled for timber, back to the mosses and the ferns?

Other thousands of us, believing that in lesser lands and common forms

Man can make forever an abundance, fought on for the still immeasurable,

still intangible needs—of Man for wilderness, of life for all its forms

and forces—to save wild beauty whole for future ages and keep unmarred

the earth's great gestures for our spiritual use. John Muir observed:

When we try to pick out anything by itself we find it hitched to everything in the universe.

J. N. LECONTE: Theodore Roosevelt, John Muir, Gifford Pinchot and others before the Grizzly Giant, Yosemite, 1903.

A new ethic was being born: that we, the living, are now and throughout time
responsible for what happens to the earth, to man, to life.

In 1908, Theodore Roosevelt as President called a Conference of Governors, saying:

*. . . there is no question now before the Nation of equal gravity with
the question of the conservation of our natural resources.*

From coast to coast Americans heard of Conservation as "the greatest good for the
greatest number in the long run."

Still, to millions of us, Conservation was an issue vast, remote.

We did not see it coming across the woodlot, pasture, cornfield, to a sagging
doorstep and a rickety child; nor in the miles-long furrows only machines
could plow, the wheatfields horizon-wide which only machines could harvest.
We did not see it, when, abandoning our hardwon farms to sink among impoverished
fields, we moved to cities, wiped soot from windows fronting on blank walls,
saw children with only vacant lots to play in, fled in summer the rooms and
pavements no night wind came to cool, took trains and trolleys to line's end,
carrying our babies and our lunches, to find only some meager green,
some dirty beach.
We did not see it when, moving out—for a breath of air, a smell of grass,
a sight of the new moon through leaves—into wave after wave of suburbs, we
found ourselves still facing windows, bounded by backyards, watching the
trees, brooks, meadows we came for vanish beneath more suburbs.
Even on holidays we did not see it when, thinking that in automobiles we had found
at last a way back to the skies and spaces, we jammed the highways,
moved bumper to bumper, inch by inch, past suburbs, industries, junkyards,
evil marshes, burning refuse, until, weary, desperate, the day half gone,
we turned off at the first shine of leaves or glint of water—and crashed
through saplings, tore flowers and branches, threw trash, polluted streams,
scared birds and beasts away from helpless young, and left unquenched
sparks that the next breeze fanned to flame.

We saw this issue, Conservation, clearer after 1929,
when the huge bubble of expansion broke.
We saw it in factories shut down, breadlines growing long, bewildered farmers
wandering homeless, their families packed into jalopies,
or trudging with a few belongings shouldered,
down highways toward some dim hope of work.
Ruin was written in the skies: from plains unwisely plowed, winds that once
stroked buffalo grass through long droughts now whirled parched soil;
dust storms darkened the sun across two thousand miles.

We saw it clearer still when Congress, led by Franklin Roosevelt, created agency
after agency to save both land and people:
—to take thin men from breadlines to build roads, schools, libraries;
pale boys to work in forests, plant watersheds, clear playgrounds;
—to set up subsidies and services to help farmers keep their land,
analyze their soils, plan better planting, learn new techniques.

MARGARET BOURKE-WHITE: Contour Plowing

From these we saw arise the dream of wider and wider planning:

    —not for one farm only but for whole regions

    —not for one dam in a river's course but for a whole watershed

    —not for one fast highway, new park, slum cleared, suburb set in green,

        but for a whole city, from core to periphery, planned as a place to live.

Now, by machines, we are torn loose from earth—
        too soon, too suddenly surrendered, the arts, skills, strengths
                that were our pride as Man.
Confined by our own artifice, borne up on vast abundance and colossal waste,
Restless, disconsolate, passing in higher, faster flight
        over old arduous obstacles,
        above old bitter boundaries,
        we course across this dwindling globe that once seemed infinite,
        hoping to find some shell of civilization harboring still
                the echoes of old faiths, passions, and delights;
        we descend into the seas, scale the last dread peaks, cross icecaps, dare outer space,
        seeking somewhere, in some last far place, our birthright: the wild majesty,
                beauty, freedom through which for a million years Man grew,
        —too few of us aware that to any beauty we must come as lovers, not destroyers,
        come humbly, softly, to look, listen, learn,
                to cherish and to shield.

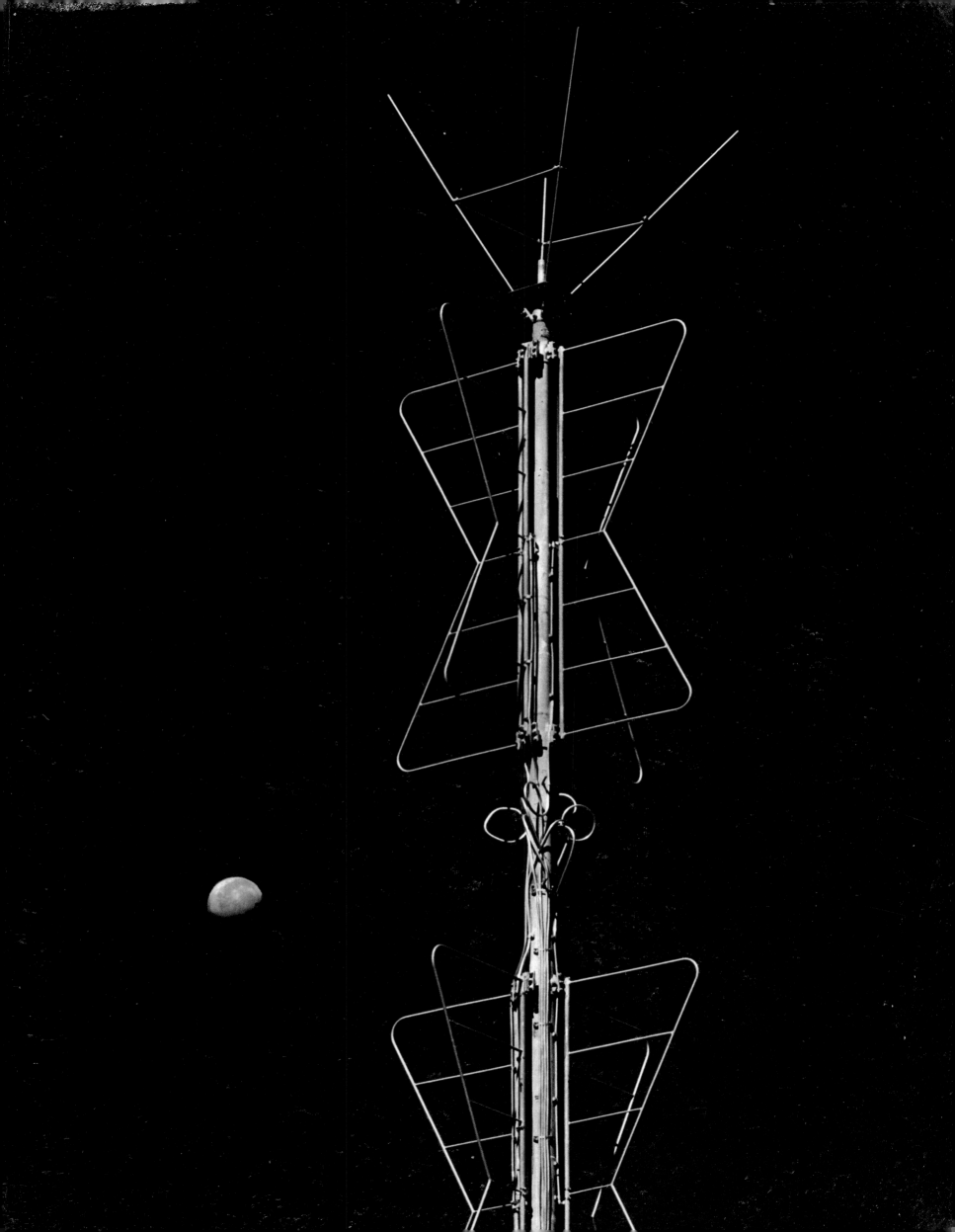

4. THE MATHEMATICS OF SURVIVAL

To St. John the Divine, on his island in the sea, appeared apocalypse;
      he saw the world as ending in the terrible glory and majesty of God.
In India, saints and sages saw, in visions vast as oceans, the world destroyed,
      the world reborn, endlessly, throughout eternity.
In medieval Italy, Dante, on a journey of the soul, saw the agonies of the damned increase
      as he descended, circle below, circle into hell,
And Milton, in Puritan England, saw archangels, hurled from the battlements of heaven,
      fall turning into devils.

Today in the 20th century, more frightful visions rise—
    to scientists tracing from present fact the cold trajectories of the future,
    and to common men and women everywhere,
    not merely by night, alone, in fear or fever,
    but by lucid day, sitting together to consider
    the mathematics of survival.

We learn to live with horrors—evils as old as man, suddenly expanded into new
    until they hang world-wide, sky-high, above our lives.
    Death rides no longer a pale horse; Death rides a ray, an atom.
    War, winged, rises on strange fires to leap oceans and continents,
        assail the moon, the sun, the stars.
    We have seen massacre swollen to genocide, tortures learned from healing.
    And, far beyond mace, thunderbolt, volcano, terrible as the sun, destruction,
        flashing immense into the columned cloud whose crown is Death.
    More dreadful than the ancient fearful riders, Famine and Pestilence, its rays,
        lingering in rock, in lethal life, its dust drifting in the winds around the world,
        dooming—perhaps already—how many forms of life
        to cancerous corruptions and to monstrous births?

ANSEL ADAMS: Trailer Camp Children

WILLIAM GARNETT: *Smog*

Hell we are building here on earth.

Headlong, heedless, we rush
    — to pour into air and water poisons and pollutions until dense choking palls of smog
        lie over cities and rivers run black and foul
    — to blast down the hills, bulldoze the trees, scrape bare the fields
        to build predestined slums; until city encroaches on suburb,
        suburb on country, industry on all, and city joins city,
        jamming the shores, filling the valleys, stretching across the plains

WILLIAM GARNETT: Housing Developments, Los Angeles
Series of four aerial photographs.

—to build highways hypnotic in their monotony, looping and twisting through cities,
      entangling in danger, noise, fumes, communities once citadels of home;
      strangling the countrysides, cutting the flow of water, the roots of trees,
      the paths of wildlife and of wind, merely to bear us glazed with
      speed, seeing only the road—

—to choke water at its sources while demanding it in vaster and vaster quantities,
      logging steep slopes so that in the heights the springs and streams are dying,
      drilling deeper and deeper wells until the subterranean
      lakes are drained so low that from the coasts the bitter sea seeps in;
      building dam after ill-planned dam where they hurt instead of help—
      submerge great chasms, drown rich farmland, destroy habitats of bird and beast,
      let salmon die before impassable falls—and where in fast-eroding
      watersheds they silt up within a generation, so that for each dying reservoir
      another valley is condemned—

WYNN BULLOCK: Erosion

HENRI CARTIER-BRESSON: *Boy in Passage, Andalusia*

to take from our young their wild free wanderings and the help of home, until,
   cheated, deluded, trapped in city corridors, enmeshed in suburbs, empty of
   heart, mind, hand, they turn their energies to evil —

to allow shortsighted men pleading specious, lesser needs, to violate our
   parks, forests, wildernesses, to herd us jostled, deafened, where only a
   few at any time should pass, and, for cheap amusements and a moment's profit,
   to ruin for all time what all time cannot replace —

to plunder this planet's crust, wasting in a few lifetimes the riches formed
   through billions of years, scraping already for poorer fossil fuels — the
   coal unknown five centuries ago, the oil untapped until last century —
   sighting already the end of certain elements: copper, zinc, lead, phosphates —

FERENC BERKO: *Bathers on the Ganges*

DICK McGRAW: Haze and Mountains from Mount Wilson, California

to breed recklessly, until every day hundreds of thousands, millions more
    crowd in among our already crowded billions
until more and more, on old and newly awakened continents, two thirds
    of the population of the world find want and hunger multiplying like
    themselves
until the needs of all these multitudes drive nations into madness—
    to raise crop yields on fewer acres by killing chemicals—
    to push back deserts, icecaps, jungles for more room—
    to mine, bore, blast; blare hate, distort the truth,
        delude and warp their people—
    to grab, exploit and murder weaker nations—
    to pursue insane chimeras of power and material ease at such a
    pace that within a century Man will exhaust the earth.

And to what shabby hells of our own making do we rush?

A poisoned, gutted planet, rolling through dark noxious air?

    — its rivers dead, its mountains shrunk to slag heaps, its last valleys

        coated to catch the dirty rains, its oceans sunk to foul and deadly shallows?

    — its continents webbed, crawling, flitting with a feeble race,

        misshapen, febrile, moved by machines, push-buttoned to thought,

        kept miserably, endlessly, half-alive by surgery, injections, rays?

    — a race that never breathed wild air, nor saw the sun shine clear,

        watched firelight dance, exulted in first snow, dreamed under trees,

        nor waded in bright seas?

    — a race that never knew delight, nor freedom, nor walked to think alone?

    — launching with its last energy its doomed and wretched seed,

        exiles without hope of return, forth into outer space —

        to seek at frightful speed, for years, lifetimes, aeons, perhaps in vain,

        for other worlds, new Edens, again to conquer, ruin, and corrupt?

PALOMAR OBSERVATORY: Crab Nebula

Is this man's future?

Is this the end of all his courage, the fiery beauty of his dreams, of his majestic goals?
Of Man Creator, Man at his greatest—poet, musician, mathematician, architect, artist?
lifting the bowed spirit, freeing the prisoned mind,
touching to ecstasy eyes that had not seen, ears that had not heard?
raising in space and sound and light the domes and spires and columns
of his thoughts?

Of Man Deliverer, Man in his noblest role—
Perseus slaying the dragon, freeing the bound Andromeda?
Hero and saint, physician, scientist
freeing humanity from early death and sorrow, from want and hunger?
To heal the wound, soothe pain, succor the weak, lend the blind eyes,
and to the cripple limbs, save mother and child from death at birth,
give all of us long life?
Who of us would willingly limit these?

And yet unwittingly Man's mercy binds these multitudes, helpless,
in crueller chains,
to face not mortal dragons but avenging angels more terrible than fiends.

In the mathematics of survival X equals Man.

This is Man's crisis.

Now is his greatest challenge.

Man Creator, Man Deliverer, Messiah, You, I—
Let us take Man's first and last resource, the fire of thought,
and with this burning brilliance, judge ourselves as Man,
and create *now* a new heaven that shall lie lightly on this earth.

Halfway between the atom and the universe,
why should not Man, in his powers and achievements,
stand at morning?

ANSEL ADAMS: Sun Halo, Death Valley National Monument

5. DYNAMICS

Shall we not learn from life its laws, dynamics, balances?

Learn to base our needs not on death, destruction, waste, but on
  renewal?

In wisdom and in gentleness learn to walk again with Eden's angels?

Learn at last to shape a civilization in harmony with the earth?

ANSEL ADAMS: *Pasture, Sonoma County, California*
(*courtesy American Trust Co.*)

ANSEL ADAMS: *Sundown, The Pacific* (courtesy American Trust Co.)

Air, water, life, these above all

— these that in their huge cycles constantly renew themselves—

these, with the sun's light, form the great conditions of Man's being.

Water for billions of years has shaped the earth—
    pouring down slopes, sculpturing channels, battering headlands,
    filling the deeps with seas, lakes and sediments that have themselves formed land.

Without water, the earth would be sharp and naked as the moon.

In water, life began; in water it evolved, until life on land
        is integral, essential, to the water cycle.
    Now water, rising under the sun as vapor, forming clouds, drifting as mist,
        cooled by night into dew and frost, falling as rain, sleet, snow,
    drips into forests and grasses and is breathed back by them into the air,
    sinks down through soil held firm by roots to fill the dark lakes underground,
        or, sparkling forth as springs, to flow in streams and rivers back into the sea.

ANSEL ADAMS: Grasses in Rain, Alaska

ANSEL ADAMS: *Refugio Beach, California*

Life is creation continuing
  —life from the lighted surfaces of seas evolving,
      form after form appearing, vanishing
  —life so ancient that sediments which death left in the seas
      and which earth's upheavals folded into the rising continents,
      now from peak and precipice confront the wind and sun

—life forever fluidly passing its earlier, cruder forms,
   forever through its new forms, born of the miracle, mutation,
   pressing with delicate filaments against harsh and hostile barriers
   seeking always the edge of the unknown—

BRETT WESTON: White Sands, New Mexico

—life indomitable, eternally changing to meet change
        pressing down into the heavier dark and cold of the sea's abyssal deeps
        pressing upward from the lapping edge of waters into air and light,
                climbing higher and higher, conquering climate after climate—

PHILIP HYDE: *Aspens, Sierra Nevada*

—life that now,

    from blind forms and sinuous phosphorescence in the ocean night
    to wings in winds above the mountains,
    weaves between the hard rock of the planet and the dark of outer space
    a veil some twelve miles deep, pulsing through water, earth and air
        with an infinity of forms
    forever bound more closely, more intricately, each to each, until
        within any place and moment, life coheres, an ever-shifting whole.

Life is severe—

the runt is not endured, the weakling falls behind as prey.

The fecundity of life is to assure survival—

into the perils of the sea a cod looses a million eggs

and into the caprice of autumn winds thousands of silk-borne seeds float

from a milkweed's pods.

Of all these multitudes only a few, the strong, may chance to breed again.

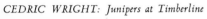

CEDRIC WRIGHT: Junipers at Timberline

What but the wolf's tooth whittled so fine
  The fleet limbs of the antelope?
What but fear winged the birds, and hunger
  Jewelled with such eyes the great goshawk's head?
                              —Robinson Jeffers

Forever the forms survival chooses become more beautiful, sensitive, diverse.

CEDRIC WRIGHT: Newborn Fawn

To birth, death is a force reciprocal.
Even the soil beneath our feet is life—
—the fabric of a living chemistry so complex its final processes elude us
—the fabric of years, centuries, millenia, of living and dying
    by plants and animals moving above in the light
    by rodents, insects, worms moving below in darkness,
    by group after group of fungi and bacteria transforming
    the minerals of the planet, the gases of air and water,
    the leaves, shells, bones and flesh death discards
    on into substances life can use again.

Through all these forms—the millions visible, the countless billions of
    the invisible—the chains of life reach up to Man;
    without these, he perishes.

The destruction of a single species may shock the entire chain of life.

Thus when man sprays death from the skys, leaches from the soil its
    minerals, kills bacteria, poisons worm or rodent,
    then death becomes unnatural, a famine, an evil working slowly upward.

And where man has killed the last wolf and mountain lion, the deer increase
    until they eat the forest bare and begin to die
    of hunger, weakness and disease.
Thus too with Man, his ancient scourges gone, looming devourer,
    disproportionate to earth, threatening with his multitudes all life
    and with feebleness his kind.

EDWARD WESTON: *Cypresses and Stonecrop, Point Lobos, California*

Life and death on this planet now lie in Man's hands.

 At depth after depth we penetrate these phenomena which encompass us.

 Still beyond our grasp shimmer the ultimate truths.

 Unless we master these, how shall we learn—not to die—but to live?

What wisdom guides life's ever-changing balances?

What subtle factors work in flesh and spirit to cause one kind to rise

 to dominance and brilliance while its near kin declines into extinction?

After overuse by Man, the earth remains barren.

Yet after vast natural disasters—earthquakes and tidal waves, fires,

 volcanos, glaciers, hurricanes—life builds back, if undisturbed by

 Man, stage upon stage, to richness.

What are the forces of renewal?

ANSEL ADAMS: *Buck*

Only the source of life can tell us—

—only the living wilderness, where Man treads light and silent as any other

—where duck and hawk belong to the same sky, and the shrill music of
    coyotes to the rims of moonlight

—where metamorphosis more strange than dreams call from the tadpole
    legs and from the dark worm in the chrysalis bright wings

—where across oceans and hemispheres bird, fish and beast follow
    paths older than the continents.

Are these mysteries we may penetrate or miracles we may only revere?

The wilderness holds answers to more questions than we yet know how to ask.

ANSEL ADAMS: *Nest*

WILLIAM GARNETT: *Flight of Pelicans over the Sun's Reflection, Gulf of Mexico*

63

ANSEL ADAMS: *The Tuolumne River, Yosemite National Park*

What, to continue their renewal,
    do air, water, life require of Man?
— Only that below the snows and glaciers of peaks, the alpine meadows
    and trees at timberline on precarious slopes face storms and meltings undisturbed
    and here no mouse, nor eagle, no wolf nor antelope, snake nor butterfly
    be hindered from his errand.

—Only that on lower spines and ridges forests stand sentinel in the rains
  and Man take from them only their abundance.
—Only that lakes lie cool and pure, and rivers brim their banks yearlong
  running clear and stainless from spring to estuary.
—Only that grasslands wave deep even under late summer suns,
  and field and orchard be so cared for that a thousand years shall but
  increase their richness.

ANSEL ADAMS: Orchard, Santa Clara Valley, California
(courtesy American Trust Co.)

—Only that Man use water wisely, to help life and be helped by it.

ANSEL ADAMS: Irrigation, Salinas Valley, California
(courtesy American Trust Co.)

ANSEL ADAMS: Shasta Dam, California
(courtesy American Trust Co.)

—Only that in cities air and light be clear and enough leaves
    remain to shadow a living land.
—Only that in each rise of land, each fall of water, each form
    of life, Man sense its character, its function in the whole,
    love it, and learn its ways, and when we turn it to our use,
    plan with inspired skills to fit to it our habitations
    and our needs to enhance—not to obliterate—its beauty?

ANSEL ADAMS: *San Francisco from TV Hill*
(courtesy American Trust Co.)

How little, from the resources unrenewable by Man, cost the things of
        greatest value—
    wild beauty, peace, health and love,
    music and all testaments of spirit!
How simple our basic needs—
    a little food, sun, air, water, shelter, warmth and sleep!
How lightly might this earth bear Man forever!

EDWARD WESTON: Grasses Beside the Pacific, California

6. THE CRUCIAL RESOURCE

Of all resources, the most crucial is Man's spirit.

    Not dulled, nor lulled, supine, secure, replete, does Man create,

    But out of stern challenge, in sharp excitement, with a burning joy.

Man is the hunter still,

    though his quarry be a hope, a mystery, a dream.

From what immortal hungers, what sudden sight of the unknown,
    surges that desire?
What flint of fact, what kindling light of art or far horizon,
    ignites that spark?
What cry, what music, what strange beauty, strikes that resonance?
    On these hangs the future of the world.

GERRY SHARPE: Boy and Horns

Pristine forever, now and for the unborn,
      let us keep these miracles, these splendors;
Pristine forever, these sources of Man's spirit, symbols
      of his goals, landscapes eternally of freedom.
Pristine forever, our ancient, basic right to know—
      to know through every sense of body, mind, heart,
      reaching from finite to the infinite,
      through every note and modulation
      of this instrument
      we for a time inhabit—
the great experience that is matrix of all others.

ANSEL ADAMS: Tenaya Lake, Yosemite

75

Shall we not come as pilgrims to these sanctuaries?
        limit, where need exists, our numbers,
        that each may find a singing solitude and pass
        free as a cloud's shadow?
Shall we not leave behind, below, tensions and frenzies,
        the cacophony of machines and fractured time?
Shall we not strip to essential skills,
        embrace the deep simplicities?
Be heir once more of all light's splendor, back in diurnal time,
        time of the turning earth and of the rising stars?
Approach, humbly and on foot — in joy — the thresholds of heaven?

ANSEL ADAMS: *Dogwood, Yosemite Valley*

ANSEL ADAMS: Trees, Illilouette Ridge, Yosemite National Park

To the primal wonders no road can ever lead; they are not so won.

To know them you shall leave road and roof behind;

you shall go light and spare.

You shall win them yourself, in sweat, sun, laughter,

in dust and rain, with only a few companions.

You shall know the night — its space, its light, its music.

You shall see earth sink in darkness and the universe appear.

No roof shall shut you from the presence of the moon.

You shall see mountains rise in the transparent shadow before dawn.

You shall see — and feel! — first light, and hear a ripple in the stillness.

ANSEL ADAMS: *Frozen Lake and Cliffs, Sequoia National Park*

ANSEL ADAMS: Dawn, Mount Whitney

79

You shall enter the living shelter of the forest.
You shall walk where only the wind has walked before.

ANSEL ADAMS: *Child in Mountain Meadow, Yosemite*

ANSEL ADAMS: Stehekin River Forest, Northern Cascades

ANSEL ADAMS: *Yosemite Falls*

ANSEL ADAMS: *Stump and Mist, Northern Cascades, Washington*

You shall know immensity,
and see continuing the primeval forces of the world.
You shall know not one small segment but the whole of life,
strange, miraculous, living, dying, changing.

You shall face immortal challenges; you shall dare,
    delighting, to pit your skill, courage, and wisdom
    against colossal facts
You shall live lifted up in light;
    you shall move among clouds.
You shall see storms arise, and, drenched and deafened,
    shall exult in them.
You shall top a rise and behold creation.
And you shall need the tongues of angels
    to tell what you have seen.

ANSEL ADAMS: Winter Storm, Yosemite

85

Were all learning lost, all music stilled,
Man, if these resources still remained to him,
could again hear singing in himself
and rebuild anew the habitations of his thought.

Tenderly now let all men turn to the earth.

ANSEL ADAMS: Aspens, New Mexico
(courtesy Polaroid Corporation)